100
GREETINGS
ABOUT TEXAS

Glenn Dromgoole

The Great Texas Line Press
Fort Worth, Texas

For bulk sales and wholesale inquiries, contact:
Great Texas Line Press
Post Office Box 11105
Fort Worth, Texas 76110

greattexas@hotmail.com
Tel. (800)73TEXAS

ISBN #1-892588-29-3

Cover Design: Jared Stone
Line Illustrations: Alexandria Collier
Dingbats: J.D. Crowe
Layout: Debbie Ford

Visit our Website to see the entire line of regional humor
books, recipe collections and travel guides.
www.greattexaslinepress.com

THE REPUBLIC FOR WHICH IT STANDS

Texas was once an independent nation,
and most of the time we act like it still is.

LIKE A WHOLE 'NUTHER COUNTRY

In Texas, we have our own distinctive music,
literature, language, food, customs, history,
geography, folklore and jokes.
Oh, yes, and lies—
except we call them tall tales.

3

LOTS OF 'EM

We have miles and miles
of miles and miles.

'DJOO SAY SOMETHIN'?

We don't talk funny.
Ever'body else does.

DRESS CODE

You can dress in boots and jeans
for virtually any occasion.
Or not.

ESPECIALLY AT RODEOS

You don't have to go far to see a real cowboy or cowgirl—or to pretend that you're one.

MUST BE A GOOD 'UN

You can tell a place that serves great chicken fried steak by the number of pickups parked outside.

ON THE HOUSE

There are more than fifty wineries
in the state, and most of them offer samples.

FIXIN' TO

"Fixin' to" is the state verb of Texas.

AND PICKUP TRUCK COMMERCIALS

Texas leads the nation in pickup truck sales.

FIRST THANKSGIVING

Texas lays claim to having the first
Thanksgiving feast—in 1598 near
what is now El Paso—twenty three years
before the one in Massachusetts.

A TOAST

As you might suspect, Texas toast was
invented in Texas.

BIGGER'N FRANCE

Texas is larger than every European country except Russia.

WORLD'S LARGEST

Texas claims the world's largest
rose garden (Tyler),
parking lot (DFW Airport),
rattlesnake roundup (Sweetwater),
jackrabbit statue (Odessa),
and fire hydrant (Beaumont).

WORLD'S SMALLEST

We also have the smallest Catholic church in the world (Warrenton).

NATIVE TEXAN

The horned toad, like some other native Texans, can puff itself up to twice its normal size.

WITHOUT MUCH EFFORT

If Texas is not the biggest or best in something,
we can sure make it sound like it is.

FLYING THE FLAG

Our state flag is the most recognizable
in the country.

NOT ONE OF THOSE SQUARE STATES

Texas has the most distinctive shape
of any state.

YOU SAY YOU'RE FROM TEXAS

When you tell someone from another state
or country that you're from Texas, it invariably
causes a reaction. Sometimes positive.

EAT UP, DRINK UP

Our barbecue is tastier, our Mexican food spicier, our catfish crispier, our beer colder.

THAT'S A FACT

Texans say it ain't braggin' if it's the truth.

SEE YA, PODNER

In Texas, riding off into the sunset
takes about a week.

BIG STUFF

We have Big Hair, Big Oil, Big Tex, Big Talk,
Big D, and Big Hearts.

BIG PLACES

And Big Bend and the Big Thicket, among other natural wonders such as Guadalupe Mountains, Palo Duro Canyon, Padre Island, Monahans Sandhills, Caddo Lake, and Palmetto State Park.

BETTER GIT OUTTA TOWN
BY SUNDOWN

The reason we have so many small towns in
Texas is because somebody told somebody else,
"This town ain't big enough for the both of us."

Y'ONT MORE TEA?

A Texas cafe is where the waitress calls you "honey" or "sugar" whether you're a guy or a gal.

HEY, BIG GUY

Things have always been big in Texas—
and we have the dinosaur tracks to prove it.

HEY, BIG BIRD

We have more species of birds than other states, and we have the windshields to prove it.

AND THE MOST BULL

Texas produces the most cattle of any state.

LEADING THE NATION

Texas has more horses than any other state. We also produce more oil, sheep, rice, and cotton.

WHERE'S ZAT AT

"Just down the road a piece" or "over yonder" are standard units of measurement in Texas.

GOLIAD, TOO

We remember the Alamo.

STICKY SITUATION

West Texas women know not to wear lip gloss
during a dust storm.

HOWEVER YOU SAY IT,
WE HAVE LOTS OF IT

Texans know there are two correct ways
to pronounce the word "oil":
"all" or "oyel."

36

HIT THE TRAIL

The cowboy, as we've come to know him, grew out of the massive Texas trail drives that moved millions of cattle to market from 1865 to 1885.

NOT THE BASEBALL TEAM

The Texas Rangers trace their history back to
1823. Stephen F. Austin called them "Rangers"
because they ranged over such a wide territory
protecting colonists.

IN THE BACK, JACK

Dogs know their place in Texas—
riding in the back of the pickup.

AND FRITO PIE

Fritos, corn dogs and onion rings originated
in Texas.

GIG'EM, HOOK'EM

If you say you're an Aggie, a Longhorn, a Red
Raider, or a Horned Frog, no one has to ask
where you went to college.

TRICKS AND MARKS

The domino game of 42 was invented in Texas
and is played almost exclusively in Texas.

DADDY'S GRANDDADDY'S GRANDDADDY WAS THERE

Texas history is colorful, dynamic—and young.
A middle-aged Texas adult is only four or five
generations removed from the Texas revolution,
three or four from the settling of the frontier,
and two generations from the oil boom days.

EVEN THE KIDS DON'T MIND

Everybody ought to have a chance to get their
picture taken in a field of bluebonnets.

SAY CHEESE, NOT GIDDY-UP

Get your picture made while sitting on the back of a Texas Longhorn. Ever'body will be impressed.

Y'ALL SMILE

Other great places to have your picture taken:
Cadillac Ranch (Amarillo),
House constructed of beer cans (Houston),
Texas Toilet Seat Museum (San Antonio),
National Museum of Funeral History (Houston),
Popeye statue (Crystal City),
Peter Pan statue (Weatherford)

THE OFFICIAL TEXAS
SMALL (AND SLOW) MAMMAL

Armadillos are living proof that Texans have
a sense of humor. And that God does, too.

USS TEXAS

We have a battleship named for our state,
and it is still afloat.

ABILENE, ABILENE

Most Texas cities have at least one country
song named for them.

LEFT LANE CLOSED

We have more miles of road than any other state. And the most miles under construction at any given time.

WHERE ARE WE GOING THIS SUMMER?

You could vacation in Texas all your life
and never see it all.

SEE TEXAS FIRST

You can go to the mountains, the beach, the forest, the lake, or the desert without ever leaving the state.

Y'ONT CHEESE ON IT?

Texas claims to have invented the hamburger
(Athens), and for sure we perfected it.

STILL DRIVING

An old Texas saying goes:
The sun has riz
The sun has set
And here we is
In Texas yet!

STANDING TALL

Our monument of San Jacinto, dedicated to the heroes of Texas independence, is fifteen feet taller than the Washington Monument.

BIG SAM

The statue of Sam Houston (Huntsville)
is the largest statue of a hero in the world.

THAT MEANS 213 AREN'T

Forty-one Texas counties are each larger than
the state of Rhode Island.

WORKING UP AN APPETITE

A Texan can smell barbecue from at least twenty miles away.

DON'T MESS WITH TEXAS

"Don't Mess with Texas" isn't just an anti-litter slogan. It's a state of mind.

WELCOME, FRIEND

The state motto actually is "Friendship," not "Bigger and Best."

MARFA MARVEL

After more than a hundred years,
the Marfa lights continue to intrigue.

PARADISE, FAIRY, AND WHON

We have places with picturesque names like
Muleshoe, Old Dime Box, Cut and Shoot,
Buffalo Gap, Gun Barrel City, Bug Tussle,
Sour Lake, Wink, Old Glory, Happy, Uncertain,
Ponder, Noodle, Comfort, and Utopia.

BUTTERFLIES, TOO

Texans look for any excuse to celebrate; we even have festivals commemorating the mosquito (Clute), fire ant (Marshall), wild hog (Bandera), alligator (Anahuac), and rattlesnake (Sweetwater and Freer).

NOT TO MENTION CHILI COOKOFFS

Or how about food and fruit fetes:
onions (Weslaco), black-eyed peas (Athens),
hot peppers (Palestine), hot sauce (Houston),
syrup (Henderson), ice cream (Brenham),
gumbo (Orange), strawberries (Poteet),
and blueberries (Nacogdoches).

THINK IT'LL RAIN?

If you run out of anything else to talk about,
there's always the weather.

LOTS OF SPACE

We have the Space Center in Houston,
the Inner Space Caverns in Central Texas,
and wide open spaces in West Texas.

FRIDAY NIGHT LIGHTS

In Texas, Friday night football is not just a game. It's a symbol of community pride and honor.

67

CLAP, CLAP, CLAP, CLAP

The stars at night are big and bright.

BIG CITIES

Statistically, we are an urban state.
In spirit, we aren't.

SEVEN PRESIDENTS FROM TEXAS

Seven presidents have come from Texas—
Ike (born in Denison), LBJ, the two George
Bushes, and three who were president of
the Republic of Texas—Sam Houston (twice),
Mirabeau Lamar, Anson Jones.

WE'VE BEEN SLANDERED, KIND OF

Texans are not as rich, crude, or brash as we are portrayed in the movies. Well, most aren't.

HOWDY

We say, "Howdy, y'all." And mean it.

HOW TO SPELL IT

The right way to spell "y'all" is with an apostrophe, since it stands for "you all." But, then, most of y'all know that.

GO, TEAM(S)

Our pro sports teams appropriately reflect the state's western heritage and space-age culture—Rangers, Cowboys, Spurs, Mavericks, Texans, Astros, Rockets, Stars, Comets.

GOOD PLACE FOR IT

The first shopping center in the country
was built in Texas (Highland Park).

GREAT FLAVOR

The best way to make use of the pesky mesquite tree is to cook steaks with it.

THE TIME IT NEVER (OR ALWAYS) RAINED

If it's too dry, you can move to a wetter climate in Texas. If it's too wet, you can move to a drier climate in Texas. If it's just right, you're probably not living in Texas.

CHEERS

Texans gave the world Dr. Pepper, the margarita, and Shiner Beer.

DRIVE FRIENDLY

It's a courtesy in Texas for drivers to pull over to the shoulder to let a faster driver pass. And to acknowledge the courteous act with a wave of the hand or tapping of the brake light.

HOW MANY MORE MILES?

No matter what state you're traveling to, you're practically there once you cross the Texas state line.

80

HUSHPUPPIES, TOO

You're never more than thirty miles from
great fried catfish, especially on Friday night.

FIVE STATES, TEN SENATORS

Texas still has the right to divide into five states. But if we did that, we wouldn't be Texas.

WAY OUT THERE

Our wide open spaces have wide open spaces.

TAKE A DEEP BREATH

In less than an hour's drive from nearly
anywhere in the state, you can breathe fresh air,
gaze at the stars, and feel the stress ooze away.

DON'T FORGET THE BIG BOPPER

Musical legends Buddy Holly, Willie Nelson, Selena, Scott Joplin, Janis Joplin, Gene Autry, Bob Wills, Blind Lemon Jefferson, and Van Cliburn all came from Texas.

AND THE QUAID BOYS

Showbiz stars from Texas include:
Tommy Lee Jones, Jayne Mansfield,
Sandra Bullock, Steve Martin, Carol Burnett,
Farrah Fawcett, Sissy Spacek,
Matthew McConaughey, Larry Hagman,
Debbie Reynolds, Joan Crawford, Dale Evans

HISTORY IS FUN

The rich diversity of Texas is best represented at the Institute of Texan Cultures and the Texas Folklife Festival, both in San Antonio, and the Bob Bullock State History Museum in Austin.

AH'M HUNGRY

Texans may not always have great taste,
but we always have great appetites.

HOW BIG IS IT?

Texas boasts of the world's largest ranch (King Ranch), and also the largest medical complex (Houston).

STORY TELLERS

Texas authors love to write about Texas
and don't seem to run out of material.

TEE FOR TEXAS

Texas has more than 800 golf courses.

91

WAR HERO

The most decorated combat soldier of World War II was a Texan, Audie Murphy.

IT RUBS OFF ON YOU

If you're from Texas,
you're always from Texas.

WANNABE TEXANS

We would rather have wannabe Texans
than don't-wannabe Texans.

BUT WHY WOULD YOU?

If you read one historical marker in Texas every day, it would still take almost thirty-five years to read them all.

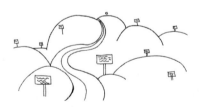

WEATHER FORECAST: ALL OF THE ABOVE

In Texas, you can have dust storms, thunderstorms, snow storms, hurricanes, tornadoes, floods and drought— all at the same time.

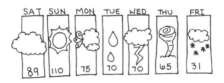

TEXAS MYSTIQUE

The Texas mystique can't be defined,
but it can't be denied.

DEMONAUTS OR ASTROPUBLICANS?

Texas residents, by law, may cast
absentee ballots from outer space.

GREAT THING

98

BACK IN 1836...

Texans are surprised to learn that Texas history
is not a required course in other states.

TEXAS IN THE HEART

If your heart's in Texas, it doesn't much matter
where the rest of your body is.

THE LAST WORD

Sam Houston gets the last word.
In a letter in 1833 he called Texas "the finest
portion of the globe that has ever blessed my
vision." That about sums it up.

ACKNOWLEDGEMENTS

Jack Waugh, Lisa Wingate, Carol Dromgoole, Lou Johnson, Ron Johnson, Kathi Appelt, Rachel Hubbard, Joe Specht, Carly Kahl, Ginger Brininstool, Rob Sledge, Don Frazier, and Robert Pace all contributed ideas for the book and provided feedback.

Published sources include *Texas Monthly*, *Texas Almanac*, *Texas Highways*, and a number of books: *Tremendous Texas* by Barbara Bartels (Premium Press America); *Texas Siftings* by Jerry Flemmons (TCU Press); *Sketches from the Five States of Texas* by A.C. Greene (University of North Texas Press); *Uncle John's Bathroom Reader Plunges Into Texas* (Portable Press); *Texas: Land of Legend and Lore* by Bill Cannon (Republic of Texas Press); *Texas* by Simon Adams and David Murdoch (DK Eyewitness Books).

ABOUT THE AUTHOR

Glenn Dromgoole is the author of more than twenty books, including *A Small Town in Texas*. He lives in Abilene and writes a newspaper column on Texas books.